Prehistoric Animals and Their Modern-Day Relatives™

Sharks Past and Present

Marianne Johnston

The Rosen Publishing Group's
PowerKids Press™
New York

Published in 2000 by The Rosen Publishing Group, Inc.
29 East 21st Street, New York, NY 10010

First Edition

Book Design: Michael de Guzman, Resa Listort, Danielle Primiceri

Photo Credits: pp. 1, 3, 10, 14, 17, 18, 22 © Digital Stock 1995; p. 1, 13 © National Geographic Society; p. 5, 8 © Amos Nachoum/Corbis; p. 6 © Henry Ausloos/Animals Animals, Bomford/Borrill T. OSF/Animals Animals; p. 8, 17 © Leonard L.T. Rhodes/Animals Animals; p. 14 © The Natural History Museum, London/Orbis; p. 18 © James Watt/Animals Animals; p. 20 © 1990 Tom Haight.

Johnston, Marianne.
    Prehistoric animals and their modern-day relatives: sharks past and present / by Marianne Johnston.
        p.   cm.—(Prehistoric animals and their modern-day relatives)
    Includes index.
    Summary: Discusses the prehistoric ancestors, evolution, and some modern species of sharks.
    ISBN 0-8239-5206-1

    1. Sharks, Fossil—Juvenile literature. 2. Sharks—Juvenile literature. [1. Sharks, Fossil. 2. Sharks. 3. Prehistoric animals.]
    I. Title. II. Series: Johnston, Marianne. Prehistoric animals and their modern-day relatives.

    QE852.C52J65 1998
    567.3—dc21   98-3879
                                                                               CIP
                                                                               AC

Manufactured in the United States of America

CONTENTS

ANCIENT FISH

When you close your eyes and think of a shark, what do you see? You probably picture a sleek fish gliding through the water. You see sharp white teeth crowding in a huge mouth and a large **dorsal fin** standing straight up out of the shark's back. These quiet creatures swim in all the oceans of the world.

The first shark-like fish lived around 400 million years ago. By the time the very first dinosaurs lived, sharks had already been around for almost 200 million years!

A modern-day bull shark swims the sea
in search of food.

SHARKS AND THEIR ANCESTORS

Today, there are more than 350 **species** of sharks that swim in all the oceans of Earth. They range from the powerful great white shark to the enormous whale shark. There's even a tiny dwarf dog shark which is only eight inches long.

The **ancestors** of sharks were not quite like the sharks of today. Sharks have changed over time. This slow process of change, called **evolution**, happens over millions of years.

The amazing thing about sharks is that evolution hasn't changed them very much. Their basic form and shape have stayed similar for 400 million years!

The great white shark and the whale shark are very good at finding food, even in the deep dark sea.

SHARK FOSSILS

Sometimes when an animal dies, its bones and teeth get buried under layers of dirt. These **remains** are called **fossils**. They help us learn about animals that lived long ago.

Learning about sharks from their fossils can be very difficult. That's because sharks don't have any bones in their bodies. Shark skeletons are made of **cartilage**, the same stuff your nose and ears are made of. Cartilage doesn't fossilize. Instead, it **decays** when the shark dies.

Usually, the only part left after a shark decays is the teeth. Luckily for scientists, each kind of shark has its own unique teeth. We can learn a lot about the history of sharks from the teeth that are left behind.

A tooth fossil from an ancient shark. ▶

SHARKS IN OHIO?

Some of the best shark fossils have been found in the state of Ohio in the United States. But if you look at a map of the United States, you'll see that Ohio isn't anywhere near the ocean.

So how did shark fossils end up there? Millions of years ago, most of North America was covered by a huge ocean. The areas where the shark fossils were found were part of a soft, muddy section of the floor in this ancient ocean.

All kinds of sea creatures that died there came to rest in the muddy bottom. Along with their teeth, the mud preserved **imprints** of their bodies.

UNITED STATES OF AMERICA

OHIO

Millions of years ago, ancient sharks swam in an ocean that covered North America.

11

AN ANCIENT SHARK

Some of the best fossils found in Ohio were imprints of the 400-million-year-old **Cladoselache**.

The shark-shaped body of this **prehistoric** fish measured almost six feet long. Its snout wasn't as pointed as the snout of a modern shark. And instead of one dorsal fin, like today's shark has, Cladoselache had two dorsal fins of equal size.

This shark was probably a fast swimmer. The Cladoselache found in Ohio and others like it were found with whole fish swallowed tail-first in their stomachs!

Picture this early shark swimming fast on the trail of its **prey**, catching it by the tail, and swallowing it in one gulp!

Sharks have lots of very sharp teeth, but they are not made for chewing. Sharks usually swallow food in whole chunks. ▶

OTHER EARLY SHARKS

Many early sharks had interesting features. **Stethacanthus** lived about 330 million years ago. It had many small tooth-like growths lining the top of its head, and its dorsal fin was topped with a flat surface that also had these teeth growing out of it. Some scientists believe these sharp surfaces were used for protection.

Hybodus was a very common type of early shark. It had two sharp spikes sticking out of its back, right in front of the dorsal fin.

By the time most of the dinosaurs disappeared about 65 million years ago, most of these early sharks had also become **extinct**.

Hybodus and other early shark species, once lived in many oceans of the world.

C. MEGALODON

One of the most fearsome sharks ever to exist was the **Carcharodon megalodon**. C. megalodon appeared about 65 million years ago.

At 52 feet long, this shark was longer than eight full-grown men lying end to end! C. megalodon had sharp, pointed teeth that grew up to seven inches long. And its jaws were big enough to swallow a small car!

Scientists believe that C. megalodon was a close relative of today's great white shark.

Great white sharks are the largest meat-eating fish alive today. ▶

MODERN SHARKS

Most of today's sharks live in the saltwater oceans of the world. But some, like the bull shark, can swim into freshwater rivers near the ocean.

The great white shark lives mostly in the waters near Australia, North America, and southern Africa. It is known as one of the most dangerous animals in the world, and can grow up to 24 feet long. This meat-eater can swallow whole seals!

The biggest fish in the world is the whale shark. These gentle giants can grow up to 50 feet long. Yet they eat only tiny fish and plants.

Sharks don't have scales like other fish do. Instead, their tough skin is made of tiny tooth-like growths. These growths could be what's left over from the sharp growths on Stethacanthus's body.

◀ *If you rub the skin of a shark, it feels rough, like sandpaper.*

19

STRANGE SHARKS

    Some pretty unusual sharks swim in our oceans. The goblin shark lives in deep waters off the coasts of Japan, Australia, South America, Europe, and Africa. It has a huge, flat snout that juts out from the top of its head. Its jaws hang below and are separated from the snout. Its skin is pale gray and is almost **transparent**.

    Another strange shark is **megamouth**. It was discovered in 1976. Very few of these round-snouted sharks have ever been studied. Just like its name says, megamouth has a huge mouth, which it uses for gulping tiny plants and shrimp.

Even though megamouth has a very large mouth, this interesting shark mostly eats shrimp!

Sharks Through the Years

Sharks have been living in our oceans for millions of years, and they will continue to swim through time. Some species of sharks have been around longer than dinosaurs lived on Earth. Some prehistoric sharks looked a lot like the ones we see today. Others looked like creatures from a creepy science fiction movie! Scientists continue to study both the sharks of long ago and today. They have a lot to teach us about the ocean, marine life, and our world.

Web Sites:

http://www.ucmp.berkeley.edu/vertebrates/basalfish/chrondrintro.html

http://www.usca.sc.edu/aedc442/aedc442001974/shark.html

GLOSSARY

ancestor (AN-ses-ter) A living creature from which others evolve.

Carcharodon megalodon (kar-KAR-oh-dahn MEHG-a-loh-dahn) An early shark that lived about 65 million years ago and is a relative of some modern sharks.

cartilage (KAR-tih-lij) The flexible material that a shark's skeleton and the human nose and ears are made from.

Cladoselache (klad-eh-SEL-eh-kee) A prehistoric shark that lived about 400 million years ago.

decay (de-KAY) A process of wasting and rotting away.

dorsal fin (DOR-sul FIN) A fin on the back of a fish or water mammal.

evolution (eh-vuh-LOO-shun) A slow process of change and development that living things go through over many, many years.

extinct (ek-STINKT) When something no longer exists.

fossil (FAH-sul) The hardened remains of a dead animal or plant.

Hybodus (HY-beh-dus) A prehistoric shark that lived about 80 to 250 million years ago.

imprint (IM-print) A mark left from something pressed into a soft surface, like a footprint in the sand.

megamouth (MEH-guh-mowth) A very rare shark that eats shrimp and plants.

prehistoric (pree-his-TOR-ik) Happening before recorded history.

prey (PRAY) An animal that is eaten by other animals.

remains (re-MAYNZ) What's left of a plant or animal after it has died.

species (SPEE-sheez) A group of plants or animals that are very much alike.

Stethacanthus (steth-uh-KAN-thus) An early shark that lived about 330 million years ago.

transparent (tranz-PAYR-ent) Able to be seen through, sheer.

INDEX

A
ancestors, 7

B
bull shark, 19

C
Carchorodon
   megalodon, 16
cartilage, 8
Cladoselache, 12

D
decay, 8
dinosaurs, 4, 15, 22
dog shark, 7
dorsal fin, 4, 12, 15

E
evolution, 7
extinct, 15

F
fossils, 8, 11, 12

G
goblin shark, 20
great white shark, 7,
   16, 19

H
Hybodus, 15

I
imprints, 11, 12

M
megamouth, 20
mouths, 4, 20

N
North America, 11,
   19

O
oceans, 4, 7, 11, 19,
   20, 22
Ohio, 11, 12

P
prehistoric, 12, 22
prey, 12, 19, 20

S
species, 7, 22
Stethacanthus, 15, 19

T
teeth, 4, 8, 11, 16

U
United States, 11

W
whale shark, 7, 19